Make Money With Your Crafts

2nd Edition

Think Outside the B
Make Passive Income With Your
Crafting Knowledge
and Abilities

by
Joyce (aka JoyceIsCrafty) Roettger

MakeMoneyWithYourCrafts.com
JoyceIsCrafty.net

Copyright © 2018 by: Joyce Roettger

All rights reserved. This book or any portion may not be reproduced or used in any manner whatsoever without the express written permission of the author except for the use of brief quotations in a book review.

The author makes no claims as to how much money can be made.
The author makes no claims as to what kind of results the reader may have.

Contents

INTRODUCTION 5

LICENSES 9

OFFLINE SALES 11

ONLINE SALES 15

DIGITAL SALES 17

TUTORIALS 21

YOUR ONLINE PRESENCE 25

MAILING LISTS 29

MONETIZING YOUR SITE 33

GETTING TRAFFIC 39

CONCLUSION 41

INTRODUCTION

When you think about making money with your crafts, what usually comes to mind? Is it making lots of inventory, renting space at a craft fair, and sitting there for a weekend trying to sell your wares? In this book I'll show you some different ways you too can make money with your crafts.

First, let me tell you a little about me. I think I was born with an "entrepreneurial gene". From the time I was in elementary school I was crocheting things and selling them. I sold potholders in the shapes of leaves; Sunbonnet Sue and Overall Sam dolls for keychains and Christmas ornaments; doilies; afghans.....

So as an adult it was only natural for me (and my sister) to sell our handcrafted wares at fairs, festivals, and craft shows. I painted and my sister made soy candles. I became a One Stroke Certified Instructor and taught painting classes. We did fundraisers for schools. We had a website and an online shop. We offered an affiliate program and had distributors in different states. We had a "brick and mortar" shop at one time.

A few years ago I opened online shops on Etsy.com, Artfire.com, and a few other online selling venues. I bought a dotcom, created blogs, and joined forums.

2018 Edit: YouTube has since changed the way their monetization works and the way I understand it you have to have a huge following to be able to make money with videos there, so I don't do that any more. I'm keeping the following YouTube info in this 2nd revision of the book though, because maybe some of you reading have a huge following on YouTube and it might give you ideas.

I created a video using Windows Movie Maker with just pictures of my crocheted butterflies. I uploaded it to Youtube.com and somehow it started getting a lot of views. At the time of this writing in 2012 that video has had over 197,000 views.

Youtube sent me an email telling me my video had a lot of views and would I like to monetize it?

Well, of course! I really didn't know what that meant, but I followed the steps to sign up for Adsense. I didn't think much of it until January 2012 when I got a check for $102.25! Ok, that may not seem like a lot, but I got excited. If I can make $100, then I can make $200!

Hmm, passive income, no making, packaging, and shipping of a product. Something working to make me money while I do other things.....Lightbulb!

I started doing a lot of research and started getting ideas of ways to use my crafting abilities to make money online.

This 2018 Edition has a lot more information about how to sell your crafts digitally, which is something I'm really enjoying.

So now I'm writing this book to share some ideas with you on how you can think outside the box and make money with your crafts as well.

Some of the links in this book and on my website are affiliate links, which means I may earn a little bit of money here and there if you use those links.

A resources page can be found on my website at http://MakeMoneyWithYourCrafts.com

LICENSES

I'm not a lawyer or accountant, so I will not give any advice here.

Always do your own due diligence and check with your local city and state for any licensing you may need, such as a retail merchant's certificate.

OFFLINE SALES

Craft shows, flea markets, festivals, and fairs are always the first thing that people think of when thinking of making money with their crafts. You can sell your merchandise outright. You can take custom orders. You can make new contacts. You can add to your mailing list. They can be very lucrative. They are a lot of work, but they can be a lot of fun. You usually need to start planning your events months in advance.

Search Google and also check out your local newspapers. Call local schools and churches and ask what kind of events they have coming up and how to rent space.

Is your event indoors or out? If you are outdoors, is a tent provided? Are tables provided? Chairs? Tablecloths? Electricity?

You will need a display. You will need to price your items. You will need to make change, so it's easiest to have everything even $, such as $5 or $10. Make more sales by giving quantity discounts, such as $6 each, 2 for $10.
Will you accept checks? Credit cards? These days there are so many ways to accept credit cards with your smart phone or tablet.

Save money by packing a cooler with water, lunch, and snacks.

Fundraisers are another way to sell your crafts. You can approach churches and school teams such as cheerleading squads, baseball teams, basketball teams....

These fundraisers work just like any other fundraiser in school. The only difference is the kids have an order sheet of *your* products, *you* make the products, and the kids collect the money and deliver products. You give the team a percentage of sales.

Wholesaling or consignment is another way to sell your wares. You can find small local gift shops and offer to sell to them at a discount for wholesale. Or they can put a display of your crafts in their shop and they keep a percentage when something sells.

Home parties can bring in more sales as well. Give the hostess a percentage of sales or let her pick out some merchandise for free. You can either take inventory already made, or you can take orders, or you can make things while the customer waits.

Open Houses with other direct sales consultants, such as Tupperware or Mary Kay, can be another great way to get sales. The consultants work together in a central location, such as an apartment complex clubhouse. They each invite all their friends, neighbors, and coworkers. It's an easy way to get your crafts exposed to more people at once.

Teaching is another way to make money with your crafts knowledge. In this case you are teaching how to do a craft of some sort. Craft stores often have classes, as well as some universities. Senior centers and parks are sometimes looking for activities. In addition to teaching, you can sometimes sell some of your inventory or supplies.

The Pros of Offline Sales is that you can get feedback on new projects and you can get cash right away.

The Cons of Offline Sales is that it can take a lot of money up front to buy supplies for inventory. If you don't have the sales you want you're kind of stuck with the inventory. I always joked that if I didn't sell anything at least I would have Christmas and birthday gifts and wouldn't have to shop.

ONLINE SALES

In the last few years online selling sites have become very popular. Online shops have lower overhead than actual brick and mortar stores. Online shops are open 24 hours a day 7 days a week. Shoppers can visit any time they want, from anywhere in the world. Examples of online selling venues are Etsy and Artfire. Both Etsy and Artfire have extensive how-to's in their forums. Ebay is another venue where some crafters have become successful. Even Amazon has a handmade site.

Basically you open a shop, create a profile, and upload good pictures of your items you want to sell. Writing a description that has the keywords used to find your items will help with your traffic. You also need to figure out how much to charge for shipping and what your policies will be.

Paypal is the one of the main payment processors of most online selling sites. From paypal, you can create an invoice, purchase postage, and print a shipping label. No more going to the post office and standing in line!

If you are a pattern creator you can sell the same pattern multiple times.

Supply shops also seem to be very popular, especially if you are able to offer low prices and great service.

Fundraisers, wholesaling, and sometimes consignments can also be done online.

Virtual home parties are another way to sell more products.

DIGITAL SALES

Digital Sales with print on demand is where I've been focusing my attention the last couple of years.

You can take a picture you have drawn or painted, or a picture from your camera, and upload it to sites to make products to sell. You don't have to make any of the products yourself and, in most cases, you don't have to pay any money up front.

Some of the print on demand sites are Amazon merch, Redbubble, Zazzle, Tee Public, Spreadshirt. You can visit my website at http://MakeMoneyWithYourCrafts.com for a list of sites.

You can even upload your digital art to Etsy and Amazon using print on demand sites. Gearbubble and Printful are 2 sites I have used.

Some things you can add your art to are tshirts, tank tops, hoodies, sweatshirts, long sleeve tshirts, dresses, skirts, leggings, socks, scarves, aprons, hats, necklace pendants, bracelets, shoes, purses, wallets, tote bags, laptop bags, phone cases, canvases, mugs, shot glasses, travel mugs, pillows, blankets, duvet covers, tapestries, clocks, lamp shades, magnets, luggage tags, baby blankets, baby body suits, bibs, pacifiers, dog bowls, dog scarves, dog tshirts, stickers, notebooks, journals, calendars, greeting cards, invitations…..and the list goes on and on.

I scanned some of the pictures I had painted and uploaded them to different items.

I love taking pictures of my dog. I love to dress him up. A lot of those pictures have been made into tshirts for myself. A bonus is that other people like them and have bought them as well.

You can take one picture and turn it into several by using different filters and effects from programs like Photo Shop or one called Smart Photo Editor. You can also find different apps to use on your smart phone. There are apps that turn your pictures into Kaleidoscopes. Those are fun!

You can also take pictures of things you have made. I took pictures of some of my butterflies and used those for Tshirts, mugs, journal covers....

One example would be if you make birdhouses you could create a pretty scene with your birdhouse, some fake birds, maybe some flowers or greenery.

No matter what you make, I bet you can find a way to take a picture of it and turn it into digital art.

Be careful with things that are trademarked or copyrighted. If you sew things with Star Wars fabric, for example, you wouldn't be able to take a picture and use that because Star Wars is Trademarked.

You can add to your media library with public domain pictures. You can do the same thing with manipulating the picture with photo editors to turn one picture into several.

There are websites that have "free for commercial use" pictures you can use. Be careful with those, because other people may be using the same images. That is one time you really want to change the picture with filters.

In addition to your art, you can add text-based images to your library. Everywhere I go I see phrases on tshirts, signs, pillow, mugs. I don't copy anyone's work, but use it as inspiration to make my own products.

Coloring pages can be created with your pictures. These can be made into books on Amazon's Create Space or sold as individual pages or books on Etsy. You can upload digital products onto Etsy that are meant for the customer to print out with her own printer.

You can create Journals, Diaries, and Planners on CreateSpace and upload your art as book covers.

TUTORIALS

Whether you consider yourself an expert crafter or not, you know how to do things. You can teach how to do things in a number of ways. There is always someone out there wanting to know how to do something, and chances are you know how to do what they are looking for. If you need ideas, go to http://answers.yahoo.com/ and start browsing the questions being asked.

You can also go to youtube and do the same thing.

Here are just a few ideas:

How to cut a pattern from fabric

How to alter patterns

How to care for a sewing machine

How to thread a serger

How to use different feet on a sewing machine

How to clean specialty fabrics

How to embroider

How to knit

How to crochet

How to read a pattern

How to work with polymer clay

How to paint roses

How to prepare a surface for painting

How to make soy candles

How to use power tools

How to sand and finish polymer clay beads

How to use molds

How to decorate a cake

How to make roses out of bread dough

How to paint on cookies

How to sand wood

How to drill holes in glass

How to clean and re-stick a Cricut mat

How to make stencils from freezer paper

How to make a purse from a record album

How to make yarn from plastic grocery bags

How to dye yarn

How to cut glass

How to make soap

Is there anything you would like to learn? Interview an expert; upload to youtube; post to your blog.

Do you have any ideas yet? Keep a small notebook and pen with you for a few days and write down ideas that come to you as you go about your day.

Here are some ideas on how to get your tutorials out there:

Make a Video

There are many ways to make videos. You can either have someone record you, you can just use pictures and your voice, or you can pay someone to be on camera for you. Upload your videos to youtube and/or your own website/blog. Windows Movie Maker is an easy way to make a video and it's the way I made my first video for YouTube that got traffic. These days almost all smart phones have excellent cameras and you can very easily record videos.

Write Articles

You can publish articles on your own website or blog. There are also many many article databases and ezines you can submit to.

Write an Ebook

Collect your articles together to make an ebook. It doesn't have to be long, a few pages is enough. There are ebook databases to submit to, as well as sites such as Amazon.com.

If you're not a writer, you can outsource your work. Http://fiverr.com is an online resource of people who will do quite a few things for just $5. Browse their site, there may be something that sparks your interest. You could offer your services on fiverr as well.

You could find PLR articles and put them together as your own. PLR stands for Private Label Rights. It's content you can claim as your own. The content may have been used by other people a few times before, so it's a good idea to change it up a bit to make it unique.

YOUR ONLINE PRESENCE

2018 Edit: Learn from my mistake and don't do what I did! I did NOT have my main joyceiscrafty dotcom set to automatically renew AND I did NOT update my credit card on my registration site, so my dotcom expired and somebody bought it and doesn't want to sell it back to me. Why did I let it expire, you ask? I got distracted with my parents' illnesses and the passing of my father from lung cancer that spread to his brain.

Whether you do business online or offline, these days anyone in business needs to have an online presence. At the very least register your own name, your business name, or what your craft is as a domain and redirect that to a basic blogger.com blog and write a few things about yourself, your crafts, and your policies.

I use NameCheap for my registration. Before pulling out that credit card, though, do a google search for namecheap coupons or namecheap coupon codes. You'll always find a coupon for up to $2 off. A dot com can be bought for less than $10 a year.

Blogger.com blogs are free and you can use them as online journals, tutorials, or just to direct traffic to your shops.

So what to write about? Here are just a few examples:

Upload pictures of your projects

Works in progress

Finished projects

Uses for your projects

Caring for your projects

How to make _____

How to do _____

(yahoo answers has a lot of ideas of what people are looking for)

Contests

Surveys

Frequently asked questions

Giving away content on your blog is an excellent way to get readers and followers. Another way is to create a mailing list. Offer something free in exchange for their email address. Have you ever heard "the money's in the list"? That's what is meant. Create a mailing list and sell to that list. But don't just sell sell sell. Offer something of value. Patterns or instructions are great things to send to your list. Periodically send surveys to your list to find out what *they* want to know.

To really expand, venture into blogs on your own hosted account. [Hostgator](#) is what I use and I've been very happy with it. Their website has extensive tutorials on how to use their various services and their support staff has always helped with whatever questions I have had.

Your email from hostgator will have the nameservers you will need to put into namecheap when you decide to host your domain.

I can register as many URL's as I want at namecheap and put them all into subdomains at hostgator for one low monthly price. They are called addon domains. You can also create unlimited subdomains and redirects.

Installing a wordpress blog on your account is really easy. Your hosting company can help you with that. Or go to YouTube for tutorials.

I always email the details of the installation to myself so I don't forget my login information. As with anything, it is best to create different passwords for everything.

Log in to your new wordpress site. You're now in the dashboard of your site. You can do almost anything in here. If you're a really creative person you can customize your blog any way you like.

Create new blog posts. Create new pages. If you go to plugins, add new and type ad codes into the search box, you can install the ad codes widget to enable you to put ads in your blogs.

Be sure to save changes.

MAILING LISTS

Which makes more sense to you:

Reader A goes to your blog, reads your tutorial, then goes on to something else.

Reader B goes to your blog, would like to read your tutorial, so signs up to your mailing list. Reader B gets reminded of you once or twice a week when you send more tutorials and offers for things Reader B may also be interested in. Reader B starts to buy things from you because she has come to know, like, and trust you.

Hopefully you said Reader B makes more sense. And that in a nutshell is why we want our own mailing lists.

When I lost my dotcom it messed up my mailing lists. So in 2018 I am in the process of practicing what I preach and am starting my mailing list from scratch.

Subtle Email Marketing

One of the most important criteria for ensuring your email marketing is subtle and will not be viewed as spam is to provide something of quality to the recipients. This may include insightful articles, interesting quizzes or other useful facts which members of the target audience are likely to find useful. When email recipients realize an email they received is offering them something worthwhile such as knowledge or information about a particular niche subject they are much more likely to spend some time reviewing the email because they will not consider the email to be spam. In addition to using the creation of this copy to convince recipients that the email is not spam, the business owners can also take advantage of this copy by providing subtle advertising. This may include product references in the articles or links to your website throughout the email.

Avoiding language which makes outrageous claims can also help to keep advertising quite subtle. Using superlatives and describing the greatness of specific products is likely to be viewed as blatant advertising. When this happens, it is not likely that readers will believe there is validity in anything contained within the email because they will believe the entire email is simply one big advertisement for your products or services.

Another way to keep advertising subtle when running an email marketing campaign is to only send your email to those who are likely to be extremely interested in your products and services. This is important because when email recipients receive an email which does not reflect their interests at all, they are not likely to take the email serious and may view the email as a blatant advertisement. However, when the email is only sent to those who share a common interest the email seems more personalized. In this case the email recipients are not likely to view every product reference as a blatant advertisement because they understand there is sometimes a need to mention products or services.

Email marketing remains subtle when the content of the email is written as though it is not coming directly from the business owner. The copy may speak about the products and services as though they are being offered by a third party. This make the advertising seem more subtle because it does not appear to come directly from the business owner.

Finally, business owners can help to ensure their email marketing efforts are not viewed as blatant advertisements by keeping reference to your own website to an absolute minimum. Most Internet users often view links from one website to another strictly as an advertisement. For this reason it might be worthwhile for business owners who are marketing an email campaign to keep links to a minimum and to carefully weave these links into even the most quite benign copy. The links should be provided as though they were only included to provide you with an opportunity to learn more about the products and not as a way to encourage you to purchase these products. It might be worthwhile to consider hiring a writer with this type of experience to ensure the copy conveys the desired message and has the desired effect on the email recipients.

If you treat your mailing list with care you will start making money by offering affiliate products or your own products.

MONETIZING YOUR SITE

Making money is the whole point of this book. **Monetizing Your Website With Adsense Is Profitable!**

How do you maximize your site?

By earning a few cents to a few dollars per click from displaying Adsense ads on it. Many are now realizing that good money can be made from this source of revenue. Try the simple mathematical computation of multiplying those clicks for every page on your website and you get a summation of earnings equivalent to a monthly residual income with that little effort you have made.

Google Adsense is a fast and easy way for website publishers of all sizes to display relevant and text-based Google ads on their website's content pages and earn money in the process. The ads displayed are related to what your users are looking for on your site. This is the main reason why you can both monetize and enhance your content pages using Adsense. How much you will be earning will depend on how much the advertisers are willing to pay. It will depend also on the keywords required. If the keywords the advertiser have chosen are in high demand, you could receive more dollars per click. On the other hand, low demand keywords will earn you just a few cents per click.

How can you start making profits out of your website using Adsense?

Sign up for an Adsense account. It will only take a few minutes of your time.

When the site is accepted, you will be receiving a clip code to include in your web pages. You can insert this code on as many pages or web sites that you want. The AdWords will start appearing immediately after.

You will be earning a few cents or a few dollars per click when someone starts clicking on the AdWords displayed on any of your web pages. Trying to earn false revenues by repetitively clicking on your own ads is a no-no. This will result in a penalty or the possibility of your site being eliminated. The money you have already earned may be lost because of this.

View your statistics. Adsense earnings can be checked anytime by logging into your Adsense account.

Once you have your account working, you may still want to pattern them to the many sites that are earning more money than you are. It is important to note that there are factors affecting how your website will perform and the amount of money it will give you.

It is a common practice that when a site earning money, the tendency is for the owner to want to make more out of what they are getting already. It usually takes some time combined with trial and error to attain what you want for your Adsense contents.

Time and some important factors that you can practice and use.

How do you increase your Adsense earnings?

Choose one topic per page. It is best to write a content for your page with just a few targeted phrases. The search engine will then serve ads that are more relevant which will then result in higher clickthoughs.

Using white space around your ad. This can make your ad stand out from the rest of your page so visitors can spot them easily. There are also other choices of colors you can use, provided by search engines, which can harmonize the color of your ad with the web page color.

Test your ad placement. It is recommended to use the vertical format that runs down the side of the web page to get more positive results. You can also try both horizontal and vertical formats for a certain period of time to see which one will give you better results.

More content-based pages. Widen the theme of your website by creating pages that focus more on your keyword phrases. This will optimize the pages for the search engines. It can not only attract traffic but also make them more relevant for the AdWords to be displayed.

Affiliate programs are ways you can make money by offering other people's products. Clickbank. Amazon, Commission Junction,and Ebay are just a few of the many many online venues that offer individuals the opportunity to sign up and promote their products. There is usually an affiliate link at the bottom of the main page of their website. A lot of sites provide special links, banner codes, and emails you can use to promote their products.

So Many Affiliate Programs! Which One Do I Choose?

Ask questions first before you join an affiliate program. Do a little research about the choices of program that you intend to join into. Get some answers because they will be the deciding point of what you will be achieving later on.

Will it cost you anything to join? Most affiliate programs being offered today are absolutely free of charge. So why settle for those that charge you some dollars before joining? When do they issue the commission checks? Every program is different. Some issue their checks once a month, every quarter, etc. Select the one that is suited to your payment time choice. Many affiliate programs are setting a minimum earned commission amount that an affiliate must meet or exceed in order for their checks to be issued.

What is the hit per sale ratio? This is the average number of hits to a banner or text link it takes to generate a sale based on all affiliate statistics. This factor is extremely important because this will tell you how much traffic you must generate before you can earn a commission from the sale.
How are referrals from an affiliate's site tracked and for how long do they remain in the system?

You need to be confident on the program enough to track those people you refer from your site. This is the only way that you can credit for a sale. The period of time that those people stay in the system is also important. This is because some visitors do not buy initially but may want to return later to make the purchase. Know if you will still get credit for the sale if it is done some months from a certain day.

What are the kinds of affiliate stats available? Your choice of affiliate program should be capable of offering detailed stats. They should be available online anytime you decide to check them out. Constantly checking your individual stats is important to know how many impressions, hits and sales are already generated from your site. Impressions are the number of times the banner or text link was viewed by a visitor of your site. A hit is the one clicking on the banner or text links.

Does the affiliate program also pay for the hits and impressions besides the commissions on sales? It is important that impressions and hits are also paid, as this will add to the earnings you get from the sales commission. This is especially important if the program you are in offers low sales to be able to hit ratio.

Who is the online retailer? Find out who you are doing business with to know if it is really a solid company. Know the products they are selling and the average amount they are achieving. The more you know about the retailer offering you the affiliate program, the easier it will be for you to know if that program is really for you and your site.

Is the affiliate a one tier or two tier program? A single tier program pays you only for the business you yourself have generated. A two tier program pays you for the business, plus it also pays you a commission on the on the sales generated by any affiliate you sponsor in your program. Some two-tier programs are even paying small fees on each new affiliate you sponsor. More like a recruitment fee.

Lastly, what is the amount of commission paid? 5% - 20% is the commission paid by most programs. .01% - .05% is the amount paid for each hit. If you find a program that also pays for impressions, the amount paid is not much at all. As you can see from the figures, you will now understand why the average sales amount and hit to sale ratio is important.

These are just some of the questions that needed answering first before you enter into an affiliate program. You should be familiar with the many important aspects that your chosen program should have before incorporating them into your website. Try to ask your affiliate program choices these questions. These can help you select the right program for yoursite from among the many available.

HostGator and NameCheap both have affiliate programs and you can choose from different colors and sizes of banners.

GETTING TRAFFIC

No matter how nice your site is, or how full your shop is, or how informative your video is, you're not going to make any money without traffic.

Social Media

Facebook, Twitter, YouTube, Flickr, Pinterest....These are just a few of the social media sites out there. Interact with people, don't just try to sell all the time. Ask and answer questions. Offer contests. Share trivia. Share quotes. Share pictures of works in progress. Share pictures of your craft area. Share pictures of finished projects. Share blog posts of tutorials that you've written. Show different ways to use your products.

Create a Facebook FanPage about your craft or shop. Use Facebook as that page to interact with people involved in your niche, or who you think may be interested in their products.

Tweet about your shop.

Put videos on YouTube.

Put pictures on Flickr and Pinterest.

Whenever possible, always put your domain name in your descriptions to get backlinks and to get readers to visit your site.

Article Writing and Ebooks

When writing your articles and ebooks always include links to your site when and where you're able.

Forums and Groups

Join forums and groups relating to your craft or to who might be buyers or users of your craft. Make sure you fill in your profile and create a signature file when allowed.

Don't SPAM the forums or groups. Add valuable content and real comments about other writers' posts. Your link to your site should be in your signature file. Readers will come to know, like, and trust you and will visit your site.

Hand out your business cards everywhere you go. Overnight Prints allows you to create business cards with pictures of your products. They have great service and are of high quality.

Wear Tshirts with your domain name on them.

Make a sign for your vehicle. If you have a die cutting machine, such as a Cricut, you can make your own vinyl letters for your own sign.

CONCLUSION

I hope this book has given you some ideas on how you, too, can start making money with your crafts and your knowledge of your crafts. You are an expert and people want to learn from you!

I wish you much success.

Joyce Roettger

Be sure you have signed up for my newsletter for ongoing news, tutorials, and programs.

MakeMoneyWithYourCrafts.com

If you found this ebook helpful, please "Like" my page on Facebook! **http://facebook.com/makemoneywithyourcrafts**

www.ingramcontent.com/pod-product-compliance
Lightning Source LLC
Chambersburg PA
CBHW030117230526
45469CB00005B/1675